PAWSITIVE THOUGHTS

From Rescued Pet Therapy Dogs

By Patricia Higgins, PhD

DAISY'S PAWSITIVE THOUGHTS

Each day in every way, I'm making the most of my life – living in the joy of the present moment. I was rescued from death row at the pound and I'm thankful for each new day of life!

I like to Wag More and Bark Less – meaning I focus on Gratitude and Joy instead of Griping and Growling!

When you stop chasing the wrong things – you give the right things time to catch up to you!

I love loving. Love makes the world go around – and the day go by smoothly!

A cuddly hug makes all the difference in the world! Hugs are things we can never give away without receiving in return!

What we think, we create! Think Pawsitive Thoughts and have a positively wonderful day!

Hearts open up when you give unconditional positive acceptance -- with a smile or a reassuring tail wag!

Even a rainy day can be bright with sunshine in your heart and soul.

Take solace and relax feeling the love and serenity of true acceptance – of self and others.

It's not so much what you say or do that counts, it's how you make people feel.

Sometimes, a kind look and gentle touch expresses love better than words ever could.

WIGGLES' PAWSITIVE THOUGHTS

Intuition is the GPS of the Soul! Turn yours on! I did when I found my way to my rescuer's home after being abandoned and injured.

Don't forget that when life seems to leave you only crumbs – enough tasty crumbs can make a wonderful meal.

Yesterday is history, Tomorrow is a Mystery, Today is a Gift, that's why it's called the Present! I love Presents…are they doggie biscuits?

When one ball flies way over ahead out of reach, be patient for there will soon be another thrown your way within your reach and better than the ball before!

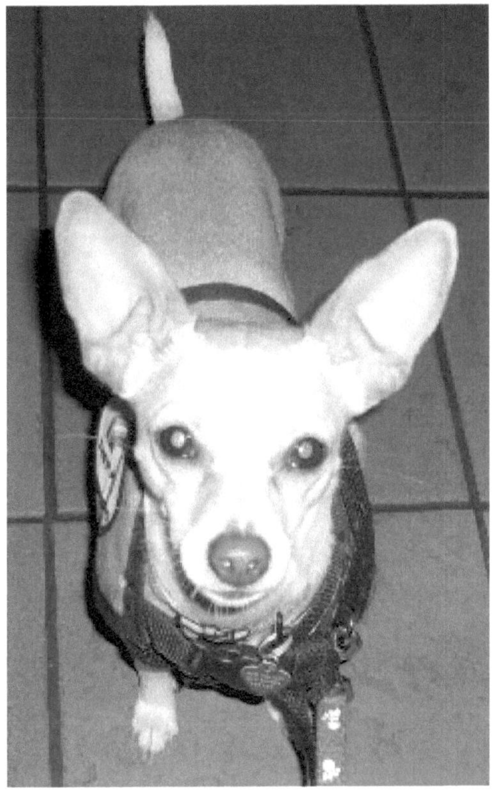

Chase your dreams…. And your friends – it's fun!

Follow your Passion…. unless your passion is chewing up carpet!

Follow your nose and your gut instinct – they'll rarely steer you wrong. What's that I smell….dog biscuits?

Even the squeakiest chew toy can sound like music to your ears…. if only you learn to listen with your heart and ears open!

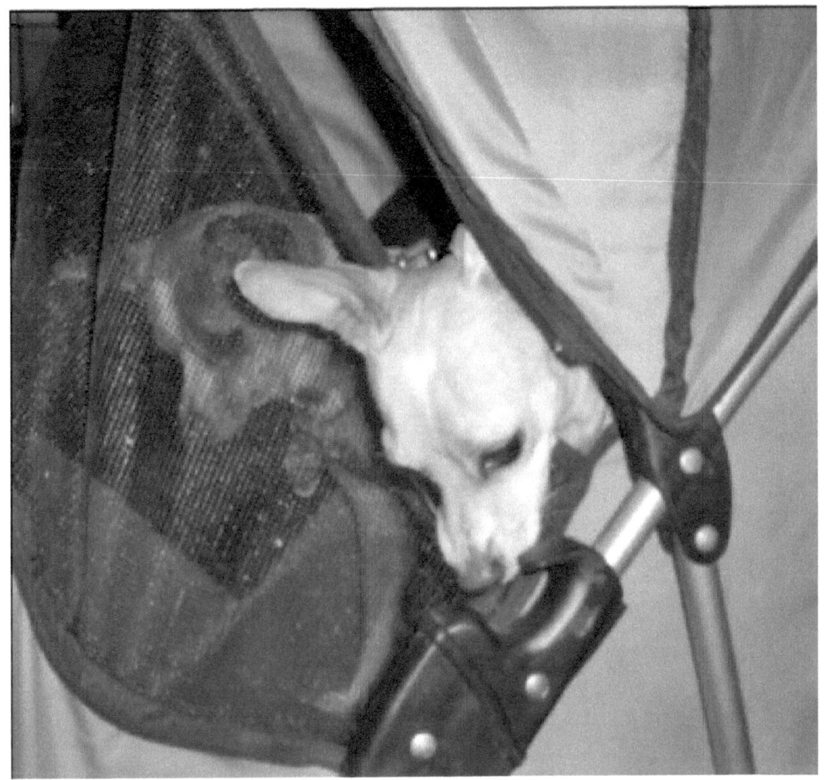

Surround yourself with good friends and play nicely together - not too "ruff".

Believe everything happens for a reason. Eventually you'll see it was all part of a bigger, better plan.

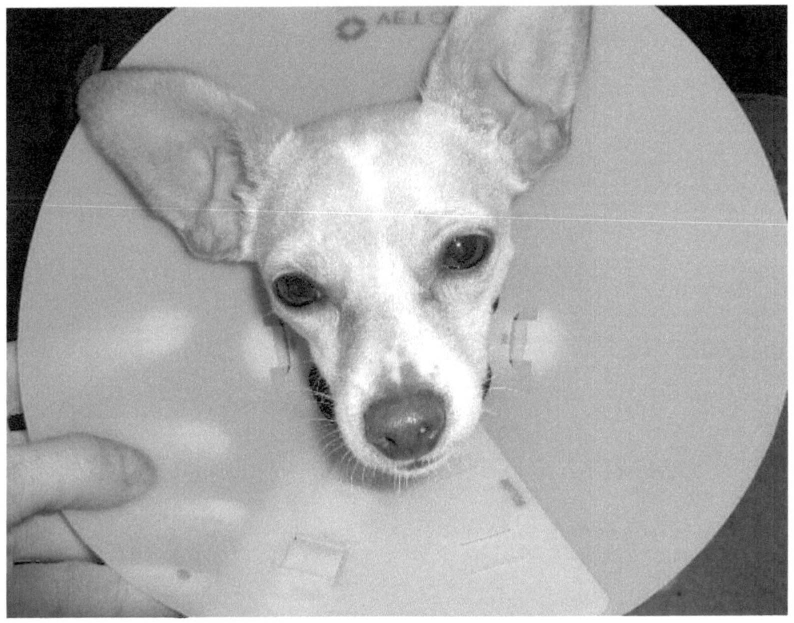

CODY'S PAWSITIVE THOUGHTS

I would never have lived past 2 years-old if I hadn't been rescued and my medical problems treated. Now, I'm the eldest at 12-years-old!

Show your appreciation and never forget where you came from and who helped along the way.

Respect your elders as they have great wisdom that can only come from experience – trust me I'm an elder!

Count the stars, but don't miss the moon! Keep your focus on the Big Picture and your eye on the prize!

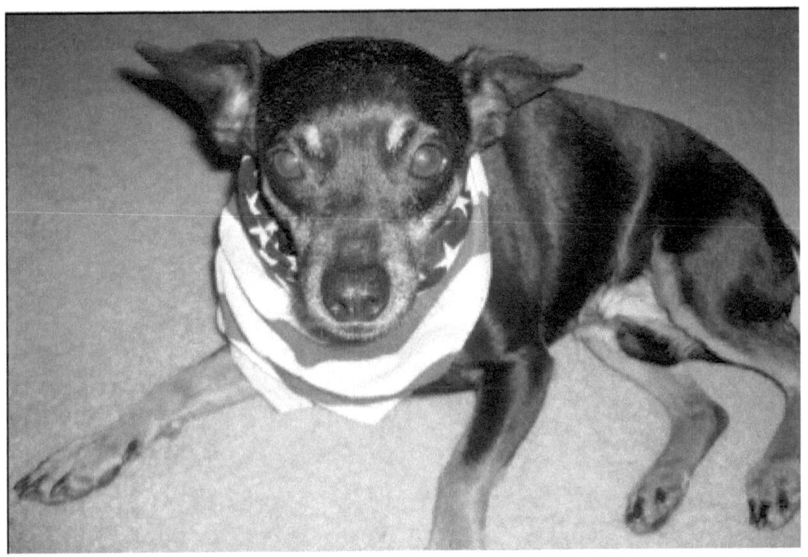

A Secret of Life is to be completely engaged in the here and now….and enjoy the PRESENT. By the way, some of the best **presents** are doggie chew toys and biscuits !

Enjoy a doggy-nap and relax in the moments of peace needed to replenish your energies – mind, body, and spirit.

Live life loving others and yourself – each day is a new opportunity to improve yourself and your relationships!

Turn your wounds into wisdom –some of the best healers are “wounded healers”.

Helping others is one of life's greatest rewards.

CASEY'S PAWSITIVE THOUGHTS

I like Synchronicity – it's like a God-incidence coincidence when things fall into place without your planning it. It was synchronicity when my rescuer stopped at a HART's (Humane Animal Rescue Team) Thrift Shop to take a break from a long road trip and found me there!

Your mind is like a parachute – open it so it can work properly!

In giving, we receive. In order to get, you have to give. So give lots of love, time, respect…. oh yeah, you could also give doggie treats…

True Trust and Faith leave little room for Fear or Worry. Worrying about the future only wastes your present!

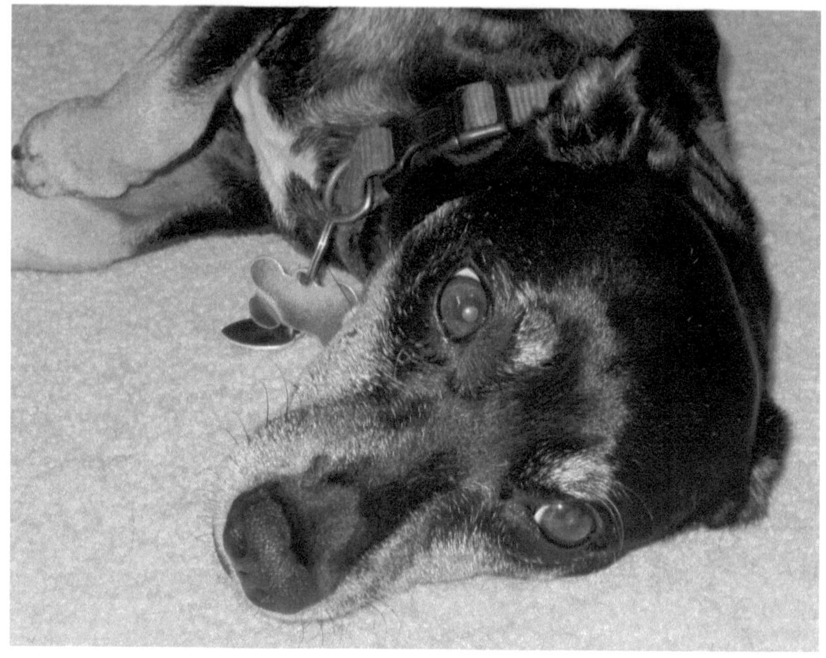

Play Time is Good for Your Mind, Body, and Spirit!

Perspective means that how you chose to interpret things affects how you'll view the situation….is the doggie biscuit box half full or half empty?

Am I lying down or begins? It's all in how you "perceive" this photo!

Flexibility of mind body and spirit helps you go with the flow and bend with curves life may throw! So stretch yourself!

What comes around goes around – so "pay it forward" by helping others and treating everyone with love and respect! Remember to show kindness and charity year-round -- not just during big holidays!

If you talk the talk – then walk the walk -- like me! Oh and wag your tail when you walk too!

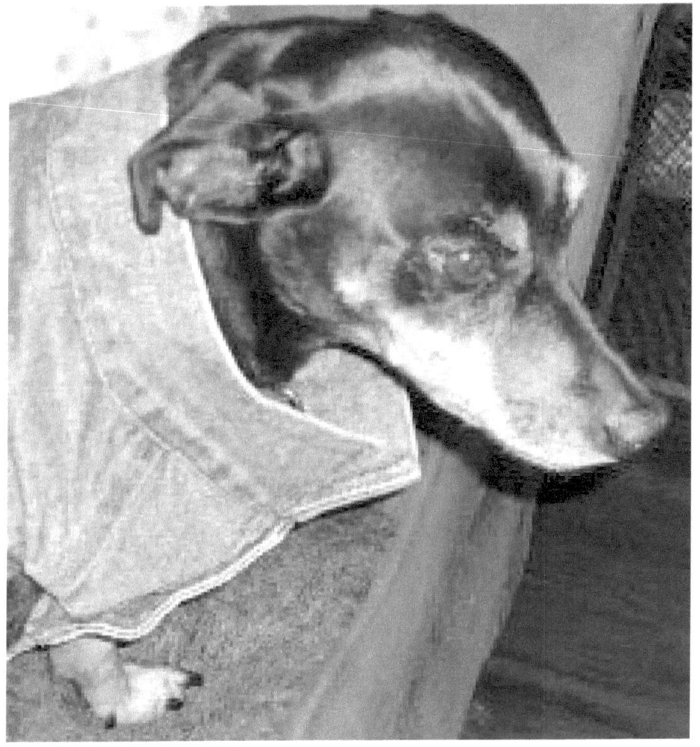

I don't think it's a coincidence that Dog is God spelled backwards! Again, it's all a matter of perspective!

See the loving soul inside of everyone you meet – you'll be surprised how good your day will go when you see only Luv and Light around you!

SPIKE'S PAWSITIVE THOUGHTS

Look for what's on the inside! Don't judge a book (or a person or a dog) by its cover. Even the dirtiest, mangiest, toughest street dog (like I used to be) can become a loyal, loving gentle pet with nurturing and patience!

If you get a second chance at life (like I did), grab it and make the most of it!

Strive for work that feels like play! That way work isn't so much work as it is play!

Nothing is as strong as gentleness, and nothing is as gentle as inner strength.

An Attitude of Gratitude goes a long way to make your day!

Going with the flow is easier and smoother than trying to go against it! Believe me -- I've tried!

It's not so much that happiness makes you thankful; it is that thankfulness makes you happy!

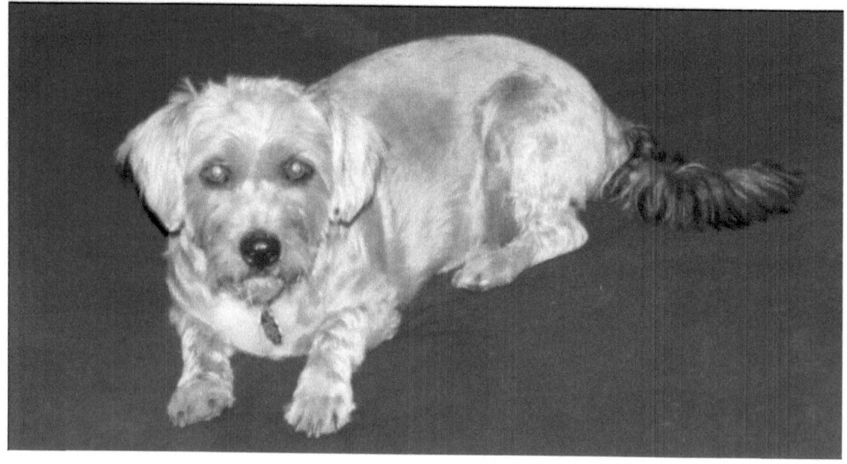

Remember – the best is yet to come and each day holds the chance to be better than the one before -- depending on your positive attitude!

Bloom where you're planted….sometimes the prettiest flower can grow from a crack in the sidewalk…and the mangiest mutt turn into a beautiful pet.

Nurture yourself and your loved ones like you would a pet!!

Give yourself lots of exercise, rest, love, healthy food, water, and don't forget playtime

ABOUT THE AUTHOR

Author, Patricia Higgins, PhD, is a licensed psychologist in CA who has provided pet therapy to many patients in nursing homes, a substance abuse rehabilitation center, and a psychiatric hospital. She first learned about the powerfully calming and mood-enhancing effects of pet therapy while volunteering with Kruisin Kritters. Elderly and infirmed patients smiled and talked happily about their own pets and the pets visiting. She saw people literally "come alive" again in the healing presence of dogs. Kruisin Kritters is an animal rescue and education program in San Diego, CA founded by Sue Miller.

Since then, she has offered patients in various settings the joy of interacting with her own pet therapy dogs as part of the therapy process. Hundreds of patients have benefitted from brief and extended pet interactions during the course of therapy. Many have expressed feelings of renewed hope, light-heartedness, and stress-reduction. The pets brought smiles to their faces and love to their hearts.

In various pet therapy groups, Dr. Higgins encouraged patients to write out their own PAWSITIVE Thoughts on paw-print cut-outs to help inspire themselves in their recovery processes. This exercise gave her the idea of creating a deck of 50 cards featuring photos of her own therapy dogs featuring positive Thoughts that could be available to the public. This book is the first step towards publishing such a deck of cards and offers 10 separate supportive, positive thoughts as if they were statements of encouragement from each of her five dogs.

Dr. Higgins credits Kruisin Kritters for teaching her about pet therapy. She also wants to thank and support Casey Mackey, a Canine Good Citizen evaluator and dog trainer, who helped establish and organize a pet therapy program at the local hospital. He also runs Mackey's Rescue, an animal rescue program in Coalinga and Priest Valley, CA.

DEDICATION & PROCEEDS

Special thanks go to Kruisin Kritters and Mackey's Rescue, two wonderful, inspirational animal rescue and education programs.

All proceeds from this-book will be donated to two animal rescue organizations equally, Kruisin Kritters and Mackey's Rescue. Kruisin Kritters is an animal rescue and education program in San Diego, CA founded by Sue Miller. By volunteering with Kruisin Kritters, this author first learned the joy of providing pet therapy to elderly patients in nursing homes. Mackey's Rescue is an animal rescue program in Coalinga and Priest Valley, CA founded by Canine Good Citizen evaluator and dog trainer Casey Mackey. Casey Mackey helped establish and organize the pet therapy program at the local hospital. Both organizations rescue animals that have been abandoned, abused, neglected, and/or injured. They save lives daily and offer second chances to pets who otherwise would not have survived. Some of these animals are adopted after being rehabilitated while others remain at the facilities and may even one day join in pet therapy programs.

For more information on these programs or to donate directly to the continuation of their programs, please contact them at:

Kruisin Kritters c/o Sue Miller
www.KruisinKritters.com & www.NaturesTails.com
1559 Campo Truck Trail, Campo, CA 91906
Phone (Cell): 619-315-4911
and
Mackey's Rescue
c/o Casey Mackey
70946 W. Highway 198
Coalinga, CA 93210B

www.ingramcontent.com/pod-product-compliance
Ingram Content Group UK Ltd.
Pitfield, Milton Keynes, MK11 3LW, UK
UKHW041838200726
13854UKWH00003BA/1202